ISBN-13: 978-0615694733 (Martin Delacroix
Publishing)
ISBN-10: 061569473X

This book is a work of fiction. Any resemblance to
persons, living or dead, or to actual events, is purely
coincidental. The characters are products of the
author's imagination and are used fictitiously.

Noah, Dane and Me

Ring-Ring.

Who's at my door? It's Tuesday night, around eleven. Is a friend drunk? Is a neighbor in distress?

Maybe somebody's lost?

I slip into my robe, flick lights on. My front door has a window, and I put my hand to the glass.

Two young men I don't recognize stand on my portico, hands in their pockets. They glance about. Their clothes are neat, they are clean-shaven, and both had a haircut recently. Duffle bags rest at their feet.

I open the door, but don't release the safety chain. I gaze through the crack.

"Can I help you guys?"

One boy, my height, slender, and dark-haired, asks, "Are you Blaise Kilgore?"

I nod.

"I'm your son. My name is Noah."

I look at the other boy. He's blond and broad-shouldered, and his face bears a blank expression.

I wait for one of them to laugh, but neither does.

I look at the dark-haired boy, and then I speak to him. "Is this a prank? Did Riley put you up to this?"

Riley's my closest friend, my law partner, too.

"Who's Riley?"

I glance at my watch. "It's late fellas. I'm not—"

"This isn't a joke," the dark-haired boy says. "I have a picture . . . ."

He produces a snapshot, one with faded colors and a crease down the middle. He offers the photo and I take it through the door opening. Stepping to a wall sconce, I study the picture. A skinny boy in a t-shirt and jogging shorts, sporting a ridiculous haircut known in the 1980s as a "mullet", has his arm around a smiling girl. In the background, Greek letters appear on a building; it's my college fraternity house.

The young man in the snapshot is, of course, me.

* * * *

The blond boy's name is Dane. They sit at my kitchen table and sip from beer bottles. Both are nineteen.

"We have no place else to go," Noah says.

Two days before, he and Dane were discharged from the U. S. Marine Corps because they are homosexual. A Camp Lejeune staff sergeant entered Noah's room without knocking. The boys were kissing, and their pants were open.

Noah tells me, "My mom and stepdad are devout Baptists. Going home isn't an option."

I recall dating Noah's mother, Lexy. The relationship lasted only a few months, as we tended to quarrel. I wanted things my way, and she wouldn't always agree. But I took her to fraternity parties, to concerts, and ball games and, yes, we had sex several times. She wasn't a devout Baptist when *I* knew her.

But people change, don't they?

I never had sex with men during college, but now I do, albeit discreetly.

Ocala's a conservative town, and I can't jeopardize my position. I can't live openly as a gay man.

Do I share this information with Noah and Dane?

I ought to be suspicious. Lexy never told me she was pregnant—she never asked for child support—and it doesn't make sense.

Why didn't she?

I should demand a DNA test, before I get involved, but I look at Noah and I'm sure he's mine. He has my wiry build, my green eyes and needle nose. Even his hands, with their long and tapered fingers, look like mine.

Dane has no family. He doesn't know who his father is. He says his mother had "addiction issues" when the State of Florida took him, at age nine. He lived in foster homes thereafter.

When Dane turned eighteen, the system showed him the street. He had no job skills and no employment prospects. The Marines seemed a logical solution, he says: three squares a day, housing, medical care and a paycheck. He speaks with a drawl, his words pour like syrup from his lips.

Dane's unabashed about his sexuality. From

time to time he'll reach for Noah; he'll stroke Noah's forearm or squeeze his shoulder.

"I fought my gay urges," Noah says. "I believed the Marines would squeeze them out of me." He doesn't meet my gaze when he speaks. His arms are crossed at his chest, and he stares at the floor.

"I lasted a year before I gave in; that's when I met Dane."

I ask Noah how he found me.

"I've known your name since I was little, when Mom gave me the photograph. The Internet's amazing, plus not many guys are named Blaise Kilgore."

I nod. "How come you didn't contact me before?"

Noah raises his shoulders. "Mom said you were a sick and selfish guy. She wanted no part of you. Why would I?"

Sick? Selfish? Me?

"Mom married my stepdad when I was three. He's been my father ever since."

"You're certain they'd reject you if they found out?"

He puckers one side of his face and nods.

I say, "People surprise you sometimes. I'm sure your mother cares."

Noah rearranges himself in his chair.

"Mom has a friend from church, Laura Tibbett. Laura's son, Gary, came out to Laura when he was sixteen, told her he was gay. Laura sent Gary to a clinic in Tennessee, one where they 'reprogram' your sexual orientation, turn you from gay to straight."

I nod. "I've heard of such places."

"It didn't work with Gary. He came home gay as ever.

"Laura met with Mom, and they prayed together; they decided Gary should go away. Gary's folks sent him to a Christian academy in the Ozarks, and he never returned, not even for Christmas."

"Your stepdad may be more flexible."

Noah shakes his head. "He's a kind man, but . . ."

I glance at my wristwatch—it's well past midnight.

I say, "Let me show you the guest bedroom."

They follow me down a hallway, and into the room, their duffel bags on their shoulders.

I say, "You can stow your things in here."
Then I point to a three-quarter bed.

"One of you can sleep there, the other can use
the living room sofa."

Opening a closet door, I reach for a pillow and
blanket, but Noah places a hand on my shoulder.

"Dad?"

I turn my head.

He says, "May I call you that?"

I nod.

"Do you mind if Dane and I sleep together?"

I look at Noah, then Dane. Shame does not
dwell in their eyes. Their breathing quickens while
they wait for my answer.

I tell myself: *They're nineteen, adults. Let
them sleep where they want.*

"It's fine," I say.

After returning the pillow and blanket to the
closet shelf, I tell them where the bathroom's located.
Then I bid them good night.

"Thanks, Mr. Kilgore," Dane says.

Noah says thanks. He tells me, "Sleep well."

I go to my bedroom, climb between the sheets, and switch off my nightstand lamp. Lying on my back, I crook an arm behind my head.

A car passes on the street and the headlights sweep my room, illuminating the ceiling. The beams cast shadows; they glide across the walls.

Conversation—barely audible—takes place down the hall. Shoes are removed, they clunk against the floor. Belt buckles tinkle, a boy yawns.

I shake my head.

Kilgore, you lunatic: You just became a father.

Now what?

* * * *

We sit in my kitchen, at my dinette—Noah, Dane and me.

We drink juice, chew toast, and gobble scrambled eggs, while coffee brews. Morning sunshine spills into the room through a window over the sink. A blue jay chirps in my live oak, and I smell a neighbor's orange blossoms.

It's Saturday morning, four days after the boys' arrival, and already we've developed routines. We always share breakfast, dinner too. The boys clean the kitchen after every meal, and they take out the garbage. They make their bed each morning. Then they tidy their room.

When I return from the supermarket, they carry groceries from my car into the kitchen, put things away.

The Marines taught Dane auto mechanics and small engine repair, and yesterday he resurrected my lawn mower; it had had not worked in two years.

Then the boys manicured my yard.

"No need to pay a gardener while we're here," Dane told me.

This morning, he studies classified ads in the newspaper. He says, "The Ford dealer's hiring, they need a grease monkey. Think I'll pay them a visit and offer my services."

I look at Dane and I see why Noah likes him. Dane's skin is unblemished and his cheekbones ride high. His eyes are abnormally large, with aquamarine irises. His lips are full, his teeth are straight, and his cleft chin juts. He wears an olive-colored t-shirt; it shows off his pectorals and shoulder muscles, his biceps too.

Dane is unfailingly polite. When I told him he could call me "Blaise", he said no, he preferred "Mr. Kilgore." When we speak he says, "yes, sir," and "no, sir." And when we dine, he won't eat until I commence. He always puts his napkin in his lap.

Noah's nervous, his eyes move constantly. He washes his hands a dozen times each day. He chews hangnails, twists his hair, wags his knees while we watch television. And he's a fitness freak; he runs six miles a day, does sit-ups and push-ups. Unlike Dane, who'll wander about my house in a pair of boxer shorts and nothing else, Noah is modest. I've yet to see him shirtless. He locks the bathroom door when he's in there and I can't imagine how he endured Parris Island with its gang showers, exposed toilets and open barracks.

Noah's favorite spot in my home is the study, a room lined with bookcases. There's a reading lamp and a leather sofa and I'll often find him snoozing there, an open book rising and falling on his chest. He favors novels: Vonnegut and Doctorow are his favorite writers.

Dane reads the sports page, nothing else.

We have reached an understanding, us three: the boys must find work, the sooner the better. They'll live with me long enough to save money for rent and utility deposits. While at my place, they will contribute money for groceries and the electric bill. I have a cleaning lady who comes weekly. She'll wash the boys' linens, but they will launder their own clothes.

Now, Noah walks to the coffeemaker and pours himself a full mug. He adds three teaspoons of sugar, then milk. He says, "During high school I worked as a busboy, then a server." He turns to Dane, "See any ads for restaurant help?"

Dane shrugs. He hands Noah the classifieds.

Noah scans the paper, chewing his lower lip. He asks about a seafood place near the Interstate highway, one offering employment.

I tell him, "It's a nice operation and the food's good."

Plucking a writing pen from a jar by the phone, he circles the ad.

* * * *

I'm having a dream. In it, Dane and I lie naked in a bed of pine needles. My mouth travels over his body. I kiss his lips, then go south, below his belly button. He moans and runs his fingers through my hair.

Above us, Noah perches on a tree limb. He whimpers like a child.

I lift my face from Dane and look at Noah.

I say, "Don't cry, son. It'll be all right."

* * * *

My law partner, Riley Perkins, shares lunch with me in our office conference room. Framed diplomas and certificates checker the walls. A plate glass window offers a view of a city park, one shaded by live oaks a hundred years old. The park's azaleas are in bloom—explosions of pink and white and mauve.

I've known Riley since third grade. We played basketball in high school. We shared a dorm room at the university two years, then an off-campus apartment two more. Riley's smarter than me and he gained admission to Duke University's law school while I attended the College of Law at Florida State University. After we graduated, we both returned to Ocala to work for the State Attorney, prosecuting misdemeanors.

Three years later, we opened our own office.

We do okay, Riley and I. He handles personal injury suits and criminal defense. I do divorce cases and probate. We both represent clients in real estate transactions; we write wills and contracts. Our office occupies part of a bank building in downtown Ocala, only two blocks from the county courthouse.

Today is Good Friday. We've given our staff the afternoon off, and we are alone in the office. I've chosen this time to speak with Riley about Noah and Dane. After I describe the situation, Riley leans back in his chair till it balances on two legs. The chair squawks in protest, as Riley's no longer the lanky boy who once played forward for Ocala High's Wildcats. He weighs two-twenty and his belly conceals his belt buckle, his neck bulges against his shirt collar.

Riley raises an eyebrow, drums an armrest. "Oh, partner, you got a situation."

I nod and don't say anything.

"I think I recall the girl," Riley says. "Dark, curly hair. Freckles and a nice pair of boobs."

"That's her."

Riley giggles. "What'll your boyfriends say when they learn you're a daddy?"

I flinch, but Riley's just teasing. He's the first person I told of my homosexuality, right after my initial experience with a man in Tallahassee. We were home from law school, Riley and I, on Christmas break, and we hunted quail in a palmetto and pine forest. We stood in a clearing, shotguns resting in the crooks of our arms, and I told Riley I was queer. He looked at me like I was crazy. Then he said, "I don't understand the gay business, but if it makes you happy, go ahead. It won't change things between you and me."

Fourteen years have passed since that conversation and nothing between Riley and me has changed. I spent last Thanksgiving with Riley and his wife, Cheryl, and their three delightful kids. Cheryl insisted I bring along Greg, a guy I dated at the time. She said, "You ought to spend holidays with your lover, plus Greg's cute; he'll look nice at the table." (Greg *is* cute. Maybe that's why he dumped me for a twenty-three year-old horse trainer.)

Now, Riley lowers his chair. Sipping from his soda cup, he smacks his lips. Then he looks at me and says, "You're certain this boy's your son?"

I nod. "When you see him you'll know. Except for his dark hair, he looks like me at nineteen."

"The hair's from his mama, I guess."

I nod again.

"You think they'll stay? Ocala's no haven for randy young men—gay or straight."

I shrug. "Guys their age don't think long-range. They'll rent a double-wide, buy used cars, maybe take a course at community college."

"The other young man . . ."

"Dane?"

Riley nods. "What's he like?"

I look at Riley. Then I blush and lower my gaze.

"What is it?" Riley says.

"If I met him in a bar, I'd try to pick him up."

Riley forms a circle with his lips, then waggles his eyebrows.

"Good-looking, eh?"

I nod.

Riley guffaws. "Oh, partner,," he says, "what a predicament. You got a crush on your son-in-law."

* * * *

Two weeks after their arrival, both boys are employed, Dane as a mechanic at the Ford dealer, Noah as a server at the seafood place.

Noah works a dinner shift three days per week, a lunch shift two other days. He works Saturday nights, but Sundays he's free.

Dane's job is eight-to-five, Monday through Friday.

Dane bought a used motorcycle on credit, Noah a beat-up Camaro.

On a warm Saturday night, Dane and I occupy my back porch. We sit on a wicker sofa, bathed in moonlight. Beyond the screens, my yard fountain gurgles, crickets chirp, and fireflies hover.

Dane wears blue jeans, he is shirtless and barefoot and I try not to stare at his rippled belly. The time's around eight o'clock.

Dane probes his gums with a toothpick. "When we showed up that first night, how'd you feel?"

I lace my hands behind my neck, then cross my ankles. "I was shocked—who wouldn't be? But things are fine now."

"If you'd known about Noah beforehand, when he was a boy, what would you have done?"

"Supported him, I'm sure. He could have visited."

"He feels bad he never contacted you."

"He shouldn't. Considering what his mother told him, I understand."

After Dane pockets his toothpick, he scratches his chest and stretches his limbs. "I always wanted to meet my dad, maybe give him a hug."

"You have no idea who he is?"

Dane shakes his head; he uses a finger to draw in the air. "On my birth certificate, in the box labeled 'Father', it says 'unknown.' When I asked my mom, she said it was true she didn't know. She'd had several boyfriends during the time I was conceived. It could've been any one of them."

Dane turns toward me, rests an arm on the sofa's back. He says, "How come *you* never married?"

I've been expecting this question. I draw a breath and look at Dane. Then I say, "Wives are for straight men, don't you think?"

Dane jerks, and then he stiffens his spine. He grins, and moonlight reflects off his teeth. "Why didn't you tell us?"

"Not many people know I'm gay. I plan to keep it so."

"Noah will be surprised."

I cross my arms at my chest, watching fireflies dart here and there. "Telling Noah may not be a good idea."

"Why?"

"He has troubles enough right now."

Dane nods, then he whispers, "Can I share a secret too?"

"What?"

He clears his throat. "I have feelings for you: desires. Is that okay?"

I look at Dane, and I don't say anything because I don't know what to say.

His eyebrows arch.

He wants an answer, Kilgore. He wants one now.

I rub the pad of my thumb with my index finger. *He's your son's boyfriend. Don't do it.*

Dane extends an arm. He teases my ear with a fingertip. Keeping his voice low, he speaks like a lawyer pleading a cause. "No one will know—not Noah or anybody else."

My heart hammers, and my breathing quickens. It's been six months since I've touched another man. Dane is so . . . beautiful.

You're weak, Kilgore. Weak and selfish.

Taking my hand, Dane brings it to his lips and kisses my knuckles.

I don't pull away. Instead I scoot over next to Dane on the sofa, so our hips touch. I place a hand on the back of his neck and pull his face to mine. Our mouths meet, our lips part, and our tongues rub.

Dane's chin stubble grinds against mine, making a scratchy sound.

We go at it like a pair of teenagers, pawing each other's limbs, our lips smacking. My cock's as stiff as a peg. After a few minutes, I pull my mouth from Dane's, and then I gaze into his eyes. They seem darker now, almost cobalt.

"This has to be our secret," I tell him. "Understand?"

He nods.

I rise and offer him my hand.

He takes it in his and gets on his feet.

I lead him into the house, down the hallway and into my bedroom. My heart's thumping so hard I fear it may leap from my chest.

Dane remains standing while I lower the bedcovers. The only light in the room comes from the hallway fixture. Seated on the bed's edge, I motion Dane to me. I run my hands over his belly and chest, and then I pinch his nipples.

Dane looks at the ceiling. When I slip a finger inside the waistband of his jeans, he flexes his fingers. Then he looks down at me and arches his eyebrows.

"Will you strip me, Daddy?"

His question gives me goose bumps.

I reach for the button at his waist; my knuckles press against Dane's taut belly. I work the button open, lower his zipper, part the flaps, and then I shuck his jeans to his ankles.

He kicks the jeans aside. His boner bulges in his briefs.

Using a fingertip, I tease his cock through the flimsy fabric, admiring its thickness and rigidity. I smell his cock cheese—a pungent aroma that makes me salivate. I peel down his briefs, and then his genitals explode into view. His uncut cock wobbles. His balls are as big as Concord grapes, dangling in their furrowed sac.

I feel him all over, taking my time. His powerful thighs are smooth, his calves are fuzzy, and his ass cheeks are firm. After I work a finger into his butt crack, I tease his pucker.

Dane groans and stretches his arms.

"Daddy, I want you to fuck me. Will you do that?"

I nod, and then I get undressed.

Dane whistles when he sees my rigid cock. "That's a beauty," he tells me. "A real cannon."

He drops to his knees on the carpet. After seizing my cock in his fingers, he examines the contours before taking my cock into his warm mouth. He goes cross-eyed while he sucks me, and his lips smack. I join my hands behind my neck; I savor the feeling of Dane's tongue caressing me. His attentions are exquisite, and so … *sensual.*

Dane slurps away in the otherwise silent room. His head rocks and his fingers toy with my nuts. He's a pro. He knows just the right amount of pressure to apply. He goes at it five minutes or so, until I place a hand on his forehead.

He spits out my cock and looks up. "What?"

I jerk a thumb toward the bed, and moments later my face is in his groin and his face is in mine. We suck cock like demons, like we're two starving men who've just been furnished a meal. I nibble

Dane's crinkly foreskin. I tease it with the tip of my tongue while I stroke his nuts and tickle the sensitive area behind his sac.

Dane groans, and then he ceases his efforts. He says, "I want to feel your cock in my gut, Daddy."

Dane lies on his back, with his head in the pillows. He holds his legs aloft by wrapping his arms around the backs of his knees. I grease his pucker with lube I keep in my nightstand. (How long has it been since I used this stuff?) His hole's tight; it flexes against my fingers while I work them in and out. The lube makes smacking and squishing noises.

After rolling a condom down the shaft of my cock, I grease myself. I drape Dane's legs over my shoulders. After bringing the glans of my cock to Dane's pucker, I gaze into his face.

"Ready?"

He grins. "Go on: fuck me, Daddy."

I ease my hips forward; I enter Dane, inch by inch, until my pubic hair meets his ass crack. Dane's lips fold back; he sucks air through clenched teeth. His eyes are squeezed shut.

"You okay?" I ask.

He nods. "It's just …."

"What?"

"You're a lot bigger than Noah."

Dane squirts a bit of lube on his rigid cock; he spreads it around. Then he looks at me and speaks in a whisper.

"Make it hurt, will you?"

I commence thrusting, and Dane grunts each time I stab him. We both sweat, and very quickly the smell of sex infiltrates the room.

Dane's pucker flexes against my cock; it caresses me, a love muscle.

He works his foreskin with a fist. "Oh, Daddy," he whispers, "it feels so good."

I bring my mouth to Dane's, and then our lips part. Our tongues rub while I work my hips. My pelvis slams against Dane's ass cheeks, making a slapping sound. A warm feeling spreads through my body, into my arms and legs and even my feet.

Dane and I have become one person, instead of two. He's a part of me and I'm a part of him. I pull my mouth from his, and then I gaze into his glittery eyes. He looks like he's high on some sort of drug. His face is flushed and sweaty.

He looks up at me and says, "I'm going to shoot real soon, Daddy. Fuck me as hard as you can."

I pick up the pace. The bedsprings wheeze and the headboard drums the wall behind it. A shiver runs up my spine and my vision blurs. A buzzing fills my head while my nuts tingle. I lift my chin and shout Dane's name. My cock throbs inside him, and then I unload, several times. My body jerks like I'm having a seizure.

A wail emerges from Dane's throat, a spooky sound. He cries, "Oh, Blaise, oh, Daddy," while his cock spurts jizz onto his neck and collarbone. He gasps for air, and his sweaty chest heaves. His pucker flexes against the shaft of my cock.

Staying inside him, I bring my mouth to his neck, and then I kiss him behind the ear. I smell his skin and damp hair. He crooks an arm around my neck and squeezes me tight.

"My god, Blaise," he whispers, "I could do this forever."

And I think, *So could I …*

* * * *

There's a lake near my house, it's a mile in circumference, and sometimes I'll walk around it for exercise. It's also where Noah takes his daily jogs. A park surrounds the lake and Muscovy ducks dwell on the lakeshore and the city provides a jungle gym and a swing set for kids to enjoy. The park is shaded by long leaf pines, by live oaks and magnolias, so even on a warm day it's pleasant.

Today is Monday. It's mid-afternoon and I sit beside Noah on a bench in the park. We stare at the lake's glittering surface, at ducks searching for bugs. Sunlight creeps through the tree canopy, it dapples the grass, it reflects in Noah's damp hair. He has just finished a six-mile run and his t-shirt is sweat-soaked, it clings to his slender torso. A breeze stirs branches of a nearby camellia, and overhead a mockingbird tweets on a limb.

Noah crosses his ankles, he leans forward and grips the bench seat with both hands. He says, "You and I are never alone, are we?"

I nod. Our work schedules—his, mine and Dane's—often leave Dane and me together at the house, but when Noah and I are home, Dane is always there. Today's an oddity. My office is closed; it's getting new wallpaper and paint.

Noah lifts his shirttail, he dabs sweat from his forehead. He turns and says, "Are you disappointed in me?"

"How?"

"The gay thing, and then the business with the Marines. I showed up without warning and now I live under your roof nearly free of charge."

"I don't mind helping. And your being gay is fine with me, don't think otherwise."

Noah's eyes glisten, he blinks back tears and his voice thickens. "I'm glad we came to Ocala, Dad. It's nice being with you."

I place a hand on Noah's shoulder and squeeze it.

Noah rearranges himself on the bench, he rests his forearms on his knees, then he moistens his lips. He says, "Why did Mom call you 'sick?' What happened between you and her?"

I'm reluctant to answer Noah's question.

Three months into my relationship with Lexy, she and I lay in my bed. Riley was gone for the weekend. I'd consumed several rum and colas and I felt reckless. While we engaged in foreplay I suggested to Lexy we try something new: anal intercourse.

Lexy didn't just say no, she laughed at me; she called me a "pervert." Her response made me angry and then I got rough with her. I flipped her onto her stomach, pinned her wrists to the mattress. I tried entering her, but she screamed so loud I had to let her go. After she crawled from the bed and got herself dressed, she pronounced me, "a freak, a crazy bastard." She left my apartment and I never saw her again.

I cringe, recalling the incident. *You almost raped her, Kilgore.*

I tell Noah, "I wasn't fair to your mom. I was troubled and angry when I knew her."

"About what?"

"I didn't understand myself or what I wanted in life."

"Do you now?"

I raise a shoulder. "I hope so."

Noah chews a hangnail, then he spits it out. Gazing at the lake, he says, "What do you think of Dane?"

My scalp prickles. I wait a moment. Then I say, "He's nice."

Noah nods, grinning at his feet. "I'm crazy about him. He's so . . . passionate."

He certainly is.

Two or three times a week, on evenings when Noah's at work, Dane approaches and kisses my cheek. He whispers, "Will you fuck me, Daddy?"

Our sex is both tender and thrilling—as good as any I've experienced—and I haven't the strength to say no. Dane's treasure I've stumbled upon. His touch is electric and almost painful it's so good.

We lay in bed one night, and I said to Dane, "I'm twice your age. What do you see in me?"

He whispered, "I never had a father. It feels good to be held by an older man."

Now, sitting with Noah, I am drenched in

guilt. He's my son, a sensitive boy and he clearly loves Dane. Me? I'm a scoundrel. Dane is too, but unlike Dane, I am no kid. I ought to know better; I should stop. I should say no, next time Dane touches me, but I probably won't.

You could say I'm addicted to Dane, that he is my drug of choice.

What is wrong with me?

* * * *

Noah and I occupy the kitchen. I chop celery while Noah peels potatoes. Tomorrow's Fourth of July and we will picnic with the Perkinses. We'll bring potato salad and baked beans. We'll watch fireworks in the park.

Dane is in the bathroom, we hear him sing in the shower. His voice is a scratchy baritone and he's *way* off key.

Noah tells me he and Dane have found a place to live, a two-bedroom trailer.

"Where?"

He describes the location—it's a rural area thirty minutes from my house.

"You'll burn lots of gas, driving to and from work."

"True, but the rent's low, much cheaper than

town."

Dane's voice reverberates off the tiles; he butchers a tune while I think of last night when I entered him, how he cooed in my ear and kissed my temple, and how he called me "Daddy."

The memory makes me shiver.

I tell Noah, "Why rush things? Why not look around some more?"

Noah grins, and then he points his chin toward the bathroom.

"What's wrong, Dad? Afraid you'll miss his singing?"

* * * *

The boys ignored my advice, they leased the trailer. They purchased second-hand furniture and kitchen stuff at garage sales. I lent them bed sheets and towels, plates and drinking glasses and coffee mugs. I bought cheap flatware as their housewarming gift, and now we load boxes into the trunk of Noah's Camaro. I have borrowed Riley's pickup and the boys' mattress and box springs, their dinette and love seat rest in the truck's bed. The time's around nine A. M., the sky's cloudless and already the sun has crested treetops to the east. The temperature's close to ninety; our t-shirts stick to us. Sweat pours from our scalps and our faces shine.

I feel lonely and depressed. It's been ten

weeks since the boys' arrival and I've grown used to living with them. It's nice sharing meals and watching TV together. I like discussing daily events over dinner. Noah's nervous energy invigorates me, it's as if he's plugged into a wall socket. And making love with Dane is . . . exquisite.

How will I stand not having him around?

Two nights ago, after sex, we sat in my kitchen in our boxer shorts, drinking beer, and Dane said, "This won't be our last time, Blaise. I promise."

I said, "I hope it's true, but your living elsewhere complicates things. We can't just hop into bed whenever Noah leaves for work."

"It's only twenty miles."

I nod, but things won't be the same, I'm sure. The distance will be an effort for Dane, he'll find excuses. If it rains or it's cold or he's tired from a day at work he won't climb onto his motorcycle and make the trip. He'll say, "Not tonight."

Now, we drive to their trailer on a two-lane county road, one bounded by horse farms, cattle ranches and citrus groves. The day's grown hotter. Under live oaks, cows lie in pools of shade, they flick at horseflies with their tails. We pass a farm, one with rows of staked tomato plants, each one lushly green. A dozen workers, men and women, Mexicans, gather ripe tomatoes, they place the crimson fruits inside cardboard boxes. They wear straw hats, long-sleeved shirts and work pants. Bright bandanas hang about their necks.

I follow Noah's Camaro. Through its rear window I watch Dane and Noah converse, their heads bob and their hands gesture. Dane laughs, he pounds dashboard with his palm and it occurs to me I've never heard the boys quarrel, not once. Their relationship seems effortless and easy, like it was meant to happen.

I once asked Dane about their sex life. I wondered, I said, if Noah didn't satisfy Dane in bed, if that was why Dane needed sex from me. But Dane shook his head. He grinned and said, "Noah was timid at first, inexperienced. Then we spent a long weekend at a Wilmington motel. We did nothing but drink beer and fuck. Noah's been a stud ever since, he'll take me twice a day if I let him."

Now, in my car on the county road, I recall a night when I rose from bed to use the toilet. When I passed the boys' room their bedsprings twanged and their headboard beat the wall with a steady cadence. They grunted like animals, and then Noah hung a dirty name on Dane. Was it "fuckboy?" Moments later, when I saw myself in the bathroom mirror, my face was as red as a strawberry.

Now my fingers drum the steering wheel. *A stud, eh?*

I'm jealous of Noah. I know it's not fair, but I am. I want Dane for myself; I want him beside me each morning.

Their trailer's exterior paint has oxidized and the siding's corroded in places. The dwelling rests upon concrete blocks, on a sandy lot behind the landlord's bungalow. No grass grows, there are no shrubs, but there are long leaf pines—thirty footers. The pines cast shadows and offer shade. Inside, the place smells musty. Synthetic paneling covers the walls and the awning windows are filthy. The master bedroom's big enough for the boys' bed but not much else. A second bedroom's barely larger than a closet. Porcelain on the bathroom sink is chipped, the medicine cabinet's rusty, the mirror speckled. The kitchen cabinets are particle board and the stove and fridge need cleaning. The carpet's worn to the weft in high traffic areas.

The boys seem oblivious to their new home's shortcomings. Dane slaps his thighs, he says, "Welcome to the Taj Mahal," while I study a water stain on the living room's asbestos tile ceiling. He says, "A bit of elbow grease and it'll be fine." He switches on a wall air conditioner and the compressor whines. The unit blows cold after a minute, and then Dane puts his face to the louvers.

"Ah-h-h," he says.

Noah lowers a box he's carried inside. Approaching Dane, he crooks an elbow about Dane's neck. Cold air blows onto his face, too.

Dane looks at Noah. He kisses Noah's cheek and says, "Welcome home, baby."

Noah beams.

* * * *

I'm at Riley's. We play gin rummy at his
dining table while sipping from beer bottles. Cheryl
and the kids have gone to a movie and we have the
house to ourselves. Drawing a queen of hearts from
the deck, I lay down a trick, a jack-queen-king
combination. I discard, and then ask Riley if I might
share my troubles.

"Sure, partner. Fire away."

I tell him about me and Dane. "It's been ten
days since the boys moved and I've seen him only
once, when they came for dinner. The separation's
killing me. I can't sleep, I've lost interest in food, and
my work has suffered. Yesterday I sat at my desk and
stared out the window all afternoon, dwelling on
Dane and how much I miss him."

Riley shakes his head. "You sound like a
lovesick teenager."

"I feel like one."

Riley swigs from his bottle, swallows. He
says, "You know that little teller at the bank? She's
blond and a bit cross-eyed?"

I nod.

"She just graduated from high school. She's
only eighteen, but I'm not lying: she flirts with me on
the elevator. She bats her lashes and touches my arm.

And I'll be honest: I am tempted; it could be fun. But, partner, kids belong with kids, don't you agree?"

I shrug. "Dane's not a child. He's mature in many ways."

Riley clears his throat. Raising an eyebrow, he speaks in his trial lawyer voice. "Shall I tell you what you *want* to hear, or what you *need* to hear."

I study the cards in my hand, riffling their edges. "Go ahead."

"Dane's being irresponsible. Your son seems like a nice young man. They're a couple, right?"

I nod.

"Call me an old lady, but cheating on your honey's not nice. And when you're doing it with his daddy it's even worse."

Riley's chair creaks. "As for you . . ."

Here it comes.

"Dane's good-looking. Even I can see that. But he's your son's boyfriend, so he's off limits. You're crossing a line."

I want to cry. My voice sounds funny. "I've never felt as lonely as I do right now."

"You must fight it, partner. Noah's your son. If you care about him--"

"Riley, I do."

"Then keep your goddamn hands off his lover."

* * * *

Days after my talk with Riley, Dane phones my office on a Friday afternoon. "Noah has a dinner shift tonight. I brought a change of clothes to work; I thought I'd come over after five. I'll grab a shower, then we can . . . you know."

Drawing a breath, I stare out a window.

"Blaise, are you there?"

"Yes."

"Well?"

I finger the receiver, chewing my lip.

I draw a breath. Then I say, "Sure, come over."

* * * *

In Ocala, in late July, it doesn't get dark till eight-thirty. My bedroom drapes are closed. Copious sunlight enters nonetheless, it reflects in Dane's chin stubble. His cheek rests upon my sternum, his head rises and falls. His arm drapes my rib cage. The tip of my nose nudges the crown of his head and I smell shampoo. He dozes and his breath whistles in his nose.

"I've missed you," he told me earlier, during our lovemaking.

His remark made my insides burn like a furnace.

Now, I scratch my chin. Shifting my weight on the bed, I stroke Dane's shoulder with a finger. I think to myself, *I've never been so happy.*

Then I hear a noise: a key moves tumblers in my front door lock, then the hinges creak.

"Dad? Dane? Where are you guys?"

Oh, no.

There's no hiding things. Noah enters the hallway. Peering into my bedroom, he sees me and Dane together, even before Dane wakes up.

* * * *

I later learned a kitchen fire closed Noah's restaurant that evening.

No shouting occurred. In fact, nothing was said. Noah turned on his heel and he left the house. He slammed the front door. I heard his engine catch, his muffler growl as he backed out of my driveway. His tires squealed on the asphalt road.

Noah's facial expression, when he saw Dane in my bed, was unforgettable. He looked like a child whose bike had just been stolen.

I've tried calling him on his mobile phone several times, but he won't answer. When I leave messages he doesn't respond. I want to tell him: I'm sorry, that everything's my fault. That he shouldn't hold Dane responsible.

I want to say, "I'm older, I should've known better."

But I can't explain if Noah won't listen.

When I woke Dane—when I told him about Noah—he became hysterical. He rolled off the bed and fell upon the floor. Bringing his knees to his chest, he wrapped his arms about his shins. Then he rocked back and forth on the carpet, howling like a lonesome dog.

He cried, "I've lost him. He'll never take me back."

I tried consoling Dane, but he wouldn't have it. Sobbing , it seemed, was necessary, so I left him in the bedroom. I went to the kitchen, and then I poured an inch of bourbon into a jelly glass. I bolted the whole thing in a single swallow.

When I called Riley and told him, he groaned.

"Oh, partner," he said, "what have you done?"

* * * *

Since that night, I have tried reaching Dane on his mobile phone, but like Noah, Dane did not answer, nor did he respond to my messages. Finally, two weeks after the incident, I visit the Ford dealership. When I speak with the service manager, he tells me, "Dane quit, he didn't give notice, even."

Taking the county road, I drive to the boys' trailer. The sky is overcast and weak sunlight gives things a washed-out look: the cows and tomatoes, the Mexicans' bandanas, all appear faded. A metallic smell of approaching rain scents the air. Thunder rumbles and lightning snakes across the charcoal-colored horizon. Wind stirs upper branches of live oaks.

Noah's Camaro isn't present when I reach the trailer, but Dane's motorcycle is. I exit my car, and then I walk to the trailer door; it's accessed by a set of concrete steps. I knock, and then I glance at the boys' garbage can. It overflows with beer bottles, frozen dinner trays, and fast food wrappers. I wait a minute, then I knock again and this time Dane answers the door. He is shirtless, wearing blue jeans, and he's barefoot. He hasn't shaved in several days. Purple crescents dust the lower regions of his eye sockets. He squints when he sees it's me, and then he lowers his gaze and doesn't say anything. He places a hand on the door jamb, shifts his weight from one leg to the other.

I say, "I called you several times. Why didn't you answer?"

He draws a deep breath. Then he steps backward. Jerking a thumb, he motions me inside. We sit on the boys' love seat, before a laminate coffee table with a brimming ashtray. The place stinks of stale beer and cigarette smoke, of days-old kitchen trash. Dane smells bad, too, like he hasn't showered lately. The room is dim because of the overcast sky, but Dane doesn't turn on a lamp. We sit in near-darkness, with our knees touching. The only sound is the wall air conditioner; it whines and hisses.

After lighting a cigarette, Dane rests his forearms on his knees.

I point to his pack. "When did you start?"

He blows a blue stream. His voice sounds scratchy when he answers, like someone took sandpaper to the inside of his throat. He says, "When Noah left me."

"He's gone?"

Dane nods and draws on his cigarette.

"Where to?"

Dane raises a shoulder.

I take a breath, let it out. "I'm sorry; I never –"

"It's my fault. I made the first move, remember?"

I don't speak for a minute. I listen to Dane smoke, watch him tap his ash. Then I say, "Why'd you quit work?"

He rolls his tongue around the inside of his lips. He hasn't looked at me once since we sat down. His gaze is fixed on the coffee table. He says, "I can't stay here; not without Noah."

"You're sure he won't come back?"

He nods. "It's clear as spring water."

Outside, thunder rumbles; it shakes the trailer. Raindrops tick against a window.

I study Dane's face, his bulgy biceps, the blue veins on the backs of his hands. I look at his feet. He trims his toenails straight across. Even at this sad moment, my crotch tingles.

I tell him, "You could live with me."

His brows gather. For the first time since we sat down, he turns his face to mine. His voice rasps when he says, "I wouldn't do that to Noah. I've hurt him enough."

I lower my gaze and my cheeks burn. *Kilgore, you are slime. This boy's classier than you've ever been, than you'll ever be.*

Standing up, I wish Dane luck. I walk toward the door, but he doesn't rise from the love seat, he stays put. I put my hand on the knob, then I turn to say goodbye, but Dane isn't looking at me. His chin is lowered and he rubs the center of his forehead with the tip of his thumb like he has a headache.

I don't speak again.

I just leave.

* * * *

Noah's letter arrives on a Saturday afternoon, toward the end of August. I read it on my back porch, on the wicker sofa. It says:

Blaise:

Or should it be Mr. Kilgore? Anything but Dad.

I've called you many things since I last saw you. None were nice, but can you blame me? You are selfish and a liar, but most of all you're a thief. You stole my lover and you stole my trust.

If I should ever become a father, I will love my son more than myself. It's a father's duty, I think, but I guess you see it differently.

The photograph of me and Lexy is enclosed.

Cody Barton

Cody Barton tried killing himself, but he failed.

Then Cody came to live with us.

His dad dropped him off on our driveway. No hugs goodbye. Dr. Barton only waved from behind the wheel of his Audi before he drove away. This was days after Christmas. The afternoon was overcast and a damp breeze fluttered Cody's shoulder-length hair while he strode up our walkway.

I met Cody at the doorstep. The rope mark on his neck looked like a violet snake; it passed beneath his Adam's apple. Dark smudges appeared beneath Cody's eyes and a few zits dotted his cheeks. He carried a suitcase the size of a portable television in one hand, his skateboard in the other. A backpack hung from his shoulders.

"Are you all right?" was all I could think to say.

Cody wouldn't hold my gaze. He stared at his feet and shrugged.

"The Bartons' housekeeper found him hanging from a rafter in their garage," my mom had told me the night before. "Some sort of family argument occurred beforehand."

Family argument? What's new?

Cody was my best friend; I'd known him since middle school. I had spent much time at his house and I knew his parents. Dr. Barton was okay: soft-spoken and reserved. But Cody's mom, Barbara, was a complete bitch. She hounded Cody about everything: his school grades, personal grooming, and even his posture. Her voice was nasally, flavored with a Georgia drawl, and I winced whenever I heard it.

When he was younger, Cody weathered his mom's insults silently. But once he'd reached high school, Cody started talking back. He argued with his mom in front of me. They would shout and sometimes throw stuff across the room. It made me so uncomfortable I avoided their home. Whenever Cody asked me to visit him there, I'd suggest another meeting spot: my house, our neighborhood skatepark—anywhere but the Bartons'.

Finally, Cody stopped inviting me over altogether.

Weekends, he often spent Friday and Saturday nights with us, sleeping on an army cot in my bedroom. My parents didn't mind; they liked Cody, especially my mom. Cody and I would sit on the family room sofa—we'd play a video game or watch a movie—and Mom would enter with two glasses of iced tea. She'd run her fingers through Cody's rust-colored hair; sometimes she'd call him "sweetie" or "handsome." Cody would grin and his cheeks would redden.

"Your mom's the best," he'd tell me.

Now, Cody followed me into the house, with his suitcase banging against his leg. In my room, the cot was already set up, equipped with sheets, a pillow and blanket. I pointed to a battered chest of drawers my dad had borrowed from a neighbor the day before.

"You can put your stuff in there," I said, "and there's room in the closet, too."

While Cody unpacked, I sat on my bed and watched. He placed his socks and underwear in the bureau's top drawer, his T-shirts, jeans and shorts in others. He tossed two pairs of athletic shoes into my closet, along with his skateboard. Then he draped a hooded sweatshirt and a jacket over clothes hangers.

The last thing Cody removed from his suitcase was a framed, five-by-seven photograph of Dean

Barton, Cody's late brother. Dean had died the previous spring, victim of a hazing mishap at his University of Florida fraternity house. Just nineteen, he died of heat stroke while locked in the trunk of a car. The beer-sotted brothers who'd put Dean in the trunk forgot he was there, until it was too late.

I had known Dean before he left for college. He captained our high school's swim team, made National Honor Society, was elected to the homecoming court. Tall and blond, with a perpetual suntan and a mouthful of white teeth, Dean was the guy all of us aspired to be. Over three hundred people attended his memorial service.

After Dean's death, Cody changed: he talked less and rarely laughed. He avoided the few friends we had. Our passion, mine and Cody's, had always been skateboarding. In the past we'd spent countless hours grinding on the streets of Clearwater. But now Cody hardly skated at all. He smoked marijuana most every evening, spent hours alone in his bedroom listening to music or wandering the Internet on his laptop computer. His school grades worsened, and some days he actually smelled bad, like he hadn't showered or washed his hair for several days.

When I confronted him about these things, Cody only scowled.

He said, "Leave me alone, Zach."

So I did.

I waited for Cody to phone me, and

sometimes I wouldn't hear from him for a week or more. He rarely slept at my house. The cot remained folded up in my closet, and I wondered if our friendship had reached an end.

Now, in my bedroom, Cody placed the photograph atop the bureau, next to his toothbrush and wallet. He stowed his suitcase in a corner, along with his backpack. The box springs wheezed when he sat next to me. Sunlight entered through a window above my headboard; it reflected in Cody's green eyes, highlighted freckles on his nose.

"Go on," he said, looking at me. "You can ask whatever you want to; I don't care."

"Tell me why you did it."

He gazed into his lap. "I couldn't take her shit any longer."

"Your mom's?"

Cody nodded. He spoke in falsetto, mimicking his mother, complete with Georgia drawl. "'Dean made Honor Roll every term, why can't you? And why aren't you dating? Dean had a girlfriend his sophomore year.'"

Cody puckered one side of his face. "Why go on living with *her* in my life?"

I scratched my head, thinking, *I smell bullshit.*

Cody's explanation didn't ring true. I was

pretty sure something else had driven Cody over the edge—exactly what I had no idea—but I didn't say anything.

According to my mom, Cody's therapist had insisted Cody *not* return to the Bartons' home after his brief stay in a psychiatric facility. Arrangements had been made between Cody's folks and mine. Cody would live under our roof, at least until school year's end, when Cody and I would graduate. Each month the Bartons would write my parents a check for Cody's food and incidentals.

Now, in the bedroom, I looked at Cody and wondered what thoughts dwelled inside his head. Was he angry his suicide attempt had failed? And how did he feel about living with my family?

Cody glanced at his wristwatch. He rose, and then he plucked a bottle of prescription pills from his backpack. After placing one tablet on his tongue, he swallowed.

"What's that?" I asked.

"Anti-depression medication."

When I made a face, Cody raised his shoulders and puffed out his cheeks.

"Sorry, Zach; I guess I'm kind of crazy."

* * * *

The day we returned to school, a band of

thunderstorms spread across central Florida. Charcoal-colored clouds filled the morning sky. Raindrops stippled the surface of mud puddles. Cody and I sat in my car at a stoplight, both of us dressed the same: beanie caps, faded T-shirts, jeans and skateboard shoes. Our backpacks rested on the rear seat.

Cody's T-shirt did not conceal his rope marks. My mom had offered Cody a tube of cosmetic cover up, but he declined it. "Everyone knows," he told her. "Why try to hide it?"

Our school had its fair share of assholes, guys who reveled in making other people miserable. I wondered what might happen during the hours ahead. How would people react to Cody, or to *me* when they saw us together?

Cody stared out the windshield at passing traffic. His voice quivered when he spoke.

"Will you walk to first period class with me? I don't think I can do it alone."

"Sure," I said. "No problem."

In the school parking lot, a few people pointed and stared. One jerk grabbed his throat; he made loud, strangling noises and his antics caused other people to laugh. Cody and I pretended not to notice. We entered our monolithic, two-storied school through glass doors. Inside, a crush of voices echoed in the hallways. More people pointed at Cody, at me too. They stared and whispered. My pulse raced and the tops of my ears burned. I kept my gaze straight ahead, avoiding eye contact altogether.

Just get Cody to class . . .

Things went okay until we reached Cody's locker. Someone had fashioned a full-size noose from a length of cotton clothesline; it hung from the finger hole in Cody's locker door handle. Cody's face turned ashen when he saw the noose. Down the hall, two guys cackled.

"Ignore them," I whispered.

A tear trickled from one corner of Cody's eye.

"I *hate* this fucking place," he said.

* * * *

On a Thursday afternoon, I drove Cody to an after-school appointment with his therapist. The therapist's office wasn't far from Oleander Park, a green space fronting Tampa Bay. After dropping Cody off, I drove straight to the park.

I'd visited Oleander two dozen times at least, and I'd always sit on a particular bench in an isolated spot. Then I'd wait for something I sorely needed: sex.

The park was a notorious "cruise area" for gay men; I'd learned this through articles published in the local newspaper. I went there after school, when my folks were at work and my whereabouts wouldn't be questioned. I met guys at Oleander who would never patronize a gay club: attractive but closeted men, some of them married.

I was queer, no question about it. I craved the feel of a man's muscles, the weight of his cock on my tongue and the taste of his semen. For some guys my age masturbation was enough, I guess. But not me; I needed another man's flesh.

Of course, nobody knew about my visits to Oleander. I'd have died of embarrassment if they had. I considered gay sex sordid and nasty, but still I craved it like some folks needed illegal drugs. Too young at eighteen to visit gay bars, I satisfied my urges at the park. I didn't feel good about myself after these encounters, but my guilt didn't keep me from frequenting Oleander.

This particular Thursday, a warm breeze blew and the sun shone, casting shadows of slash pines onto the park's sandy soil. I strode down a sidewalk, hands in my pockets, until I reached my bench. Shrubbery surrounded me on three sides and pine needles carpeted the ground. Few people were about. I crossed a knee with an ankle, sucked my cheeks and gazed at a squirrel hopping about the limbs of a turkey oak. Checking my wristwatch, I saw ten minutes had passed since I'd left Cody at the therapist's. At best I had a half-hour to kill.

I squirmed on the bench, glancing here and there. Would I fail to meet someone this visit? Would I leave dissatisfied?

Be patient; give it time.

Minutes later someone cleared his throat. I glanced toward a clump of saw palmettos. A man stood among the bushes, a decent-looking guy with dark hair and eyes, probably in his late twenties. I'd never seen him in Oleander Park before. When my gaze met his, he grinned at me and crooked a finger.

Go on, get moving.

Up close, the guy looked even better: a bit of stubble on his cheeks and chin, muscles bulging under his T-shirt, another bulge in his blue jeans. I followed him to a clearing where passersby wouldn't see us. Used condoms and damp wipes littered the ground.

He turned on his heel to face me. "I'm Todd," he whispered.

"I'm Zach."

"You're cute, Zach. Do you suck cock?"

I nodded. Already, my pulse raced. I salivated like a starving man invited to a feast.

Todd tapped his zipper with a fingertip. "I have eight inches. Want a taste?"

Eight inches? Fuck, yeah . . .

I sank to my knees. Hands trembling, I reached for the button at the waist of Todd's jeans, and then I popped it open. I couldn't wait to get my mouth on Todd's cock. While I lowered his zipper, he reached into his back pocket. I figured he wanted to play safe; I assumed he'd offer me a condom, but I was wrong.

Boy, was I wrong.

Todd flashed a badge in my face instead.

"You're under arrest, Zach."

An explosion went off inside my head. *He's a cop, stupid; you're screwed.* Then I thought, *What will Mom and Dad say?*

Oh, shit . . .

The ride to County Jail was awful. Todd and another officer sat in the cruiser's front seat, discussing banalities, while I sat in back with my hands cuffed before me, listening to their radio bark. I'd never felt more scared or humiliated in my life. I stared out my window, shaking like a sapling in a storm. Tears rolled down my cheeks. How could I have been so careless?

Things worsened when we reached the jail. The intake officer was someone I knew. Her son had performed in a school play with me and we'd rehearsed at their house a few times. She had seemed nice back then, but now she arched an eyebrow and scowled.

"Zach, what are *you* doing here?"

I lowered my gaze while my cheeks flamed.

I spent three hours sitting in a windowless cell, along with a couple of tattooed street thugs and a pale, skinny guy hallucinating on LSD. The skinny guy wouldn't stop babbling nonsense. We all wore orange jumpsuits and slip-on sneakers. I felt lower than pond scum. The cell stank of ammonia and human sweat. Above us, a fluorescent ceiling fixture hummed and flickered. I sat on a bench, staring at the concrete floor while my stomach churned. The enormity of my arrest had settled over me like a leaden blanket.

You're fucked, I kept telling myself, *totally fucked.*

My dad posted bail for me. After I changed into street clothes, I met him in the jail's reception area. He stood there with his hands in his pockets, staring at the floor with his shoulders hunched.

"Dad?"

He lifted his chin, and then his gaze met mine. I trembled like a kid in a spook house, feeling fear, disgust and shame. Why had this happened to me? Would my parents hate me for what I'd done?

Dad didn't say anything. He took me by a forearm, guided me through the exit doors and into the parking lot. The sun was down and stars appeared in the night sky. Crickets chirped among the trees. Standing next to our car, I fell apart and wept like a four-year-old.

"Daddy, I'm so sorry."

He took me in his arms and held me close.

"It's okay, son. It'll be all right."

* * * *

The night of my arrest, my parents didn't lecture me. When Dad and I got home, my mom hugged me and asked if I was okay.

"I guess," I said. "Can you forgive me?"

"We love you, Zach; this doesn't change a thing. Go take a shower."

I felt filthy from my stay at the jail. Warm water raining on my skin soothed me and helped me feel human again. But I couldn't get memories from jail out of my head: the stinks, creepy prisoners, and sordidness of it all.

Afterward, Cody and I sat in my bedroom with the door closed. I told him everything: how many times I'd visited Oleander Park, the sex acts I'd performed there, how I'd known I was gay since I was twelve, and how badly I craved intimacies with men. The words poured out of me like water from a spigot. I guess I'd always wanted to share my secrets with someone, and now I could.

Cody listened without comment. When I'd

finished talking, he tapped his chin with his fingertips. "I don't understand something," he said.

"What's that?"

"How come you didn't tell me these things before? I thought we were best friends."

"We *are*," I said, "but sucking cock's not something I'm proud of. I wasn't sure how you'd react if I told you I was queer."

Cody made a face. "That's how little you trust me?"

His remark got me angry. I spoke without thinking first. "You're a fine one to talk: you've lived here three weeks but you still haven't explained."

"Explained what?"

"The reason you tried killing yourself. And don't give me that crap about your mom. It was something else, I know."

Cody looked away and rubbed his lips together.

"Come on," I said, "tell me."

Cody went to the cot, climbed under the covers and turned away from me.

* * * *

Most everyone at school used Internet social networking, so it didn't take long for news of my arrest to spread. Altered photos of me appeared online: I'd have a cock in my mouth or a dildo up my ass. I received dozens of insulting emails, a couple of threats too. In the school parking lot, someone spray-painted FAGGOT on my car.

I was shoved and kicked numerous times in our school's hallways. Guys called me every name in the book: *fairy, fudge-packer, sissy boy, pervert* and *cocksucker*, to name a few. They made kissing sounds behind my back. People I'd *thought* were my friends ceased talking to me altogether. Suddenly I was a leper.

The only person who stuck with me was Cody. We walked to first period together each morning, ate lunch together in the cafeteria. Each afternoon we walked to my car together. None of this was easy for Cody, I'm sure. Guys called Cody and me "asshole buddies"; they accused Cody—right to his face—of being my boyfriend. But none of it dissuaded Cody from standing with me.

"If someone tries to beat you up," he said, "they'll have to fight me too."

After a couple of weeks, guys grew tired of harassing me. The insults tapered off and people stopped staring. My arrest became yesterday's news. But my former "friends" still avoided me. My cell phone rarely chimed and my text message inbox remained empty. Socially, I was a complete pariah. I went through my school days speaking to no one but my teachers and Cody.

Thank god for Cody.

Since moving to our house, he'd become more like his old self. He had emptied his bag of marijuana down the garbage disposal. He took more pride in his appearance, put more effort into school. Each afternoon, we studied in my room. In our free time we played video games, rode our skateboards and watched TV. Or we drove around town in my car, not talking much, just cruising the streets.

Our misfortunes had brought us closer together, I think. We'd both been shamed before our peers and socially ostracized. Lesser boys might've gone crazy—maybe even jumped off a bridge—but together we managed to survive. On campus we kept our grades up, our chins as well.

"Fuck people at school," Cody said. "Who needs them?"

You're right, I thought.

All I need is your friendship.

* * * *

I woke to the sound of Cody's whimpering. I'm a fairly sound sleeper, but he made plenty of noise. He lay in fetal position, under the blanket on his cot. I glanced at my nightstand clock; the time was three a.m. Cody's knees chugged, his feet kept thrusting from beneath his covers. Silvery moonlight poured into the room through a pair of double hung windows. I knelt beside Cody and shook his shoulder. When Cody didn't respond, I poked his ribs.

"Wake up."

He turned toward me, and then his eyes fluttered open.

"What is it?"

"I think you're having a bad dream."

He flipped onto his back and didn't say anything.

"What were you dreaming about?"

"The same shit as always."

"What?"

Cody looked at me. Then he returned his gaze to the ceiling.

"Tell me," I said. "I'm staying right here 'til you do."

He drew a breath, released it. "I dreamt about my brother."

"Dean?"

Cody nodded. "In the dream I stood next to the car he died in. I heard him kick the trunk lid and holler for help. He knew I was there; he even called my name. My parents watched—they shouted at me to do something—but I didn't have a key to the trunk. It was . . . awful."

"Have you dreamt this before?"

"Many times, Zach.

Jesus, I thought. *Poor Cody . . . .*

* * * *

Spring break arrived in late March. Cody and I had performed well in school, so my folks agreed to rent us a room at the beach for three nights.

"I'm trusting you," my mother said. "No drunken parties.

"And I thought, *Parties require friends, Mom. We don't have any, remember?*

But I only nodded.

The motel manager puffed on a cigarette while he checked us in. Students from assorted high schools and colleges occupied most of the rooms. Kids were all over the place, on the pool deck and in corridors. Boys guzzled beer, girls sipped wine coolers. The scent of burning marijuana was pervasive.

Our first night there, while swimming in the motel pool, we met a couple of guys from University of Florida. Ten minutes into the conversation, one guy told us the name of his fraternity and Cody's face turned white as an egg. He glanced at me and shook his head, very subtly. I cleared my throat. Changing the subject, I asked the UF guys if they might buy us beer, since Cody and I were underage.

An hour later, Cody and I occupied our room. We sat on our lumpy beds while a case of Budweiser chilled in our mini-fridge. We sipped from cans, both of us wearing only boardshorts, while Cody spoke of the boys from UF.

"I can't believe it. Of all the guys we had to meet . . . ."

"Look," I said, "they don't know you're Dean's brother."

"True, but still it's weird. They could be the ones who——"

"Let's talk about something else."

While we gabbed, I studied Cody's physique. Like me, he was skinny and pale, with a smooth chest and a narrow waist. Copper-colored fuzz dusted his calves. In one leg of his shorts, his cock and nuts bulged. The vision made me hunger for sex.

By midnight we had killed most of the beer. We lay on our respective beds, listening to reggae music on my portable player. I didn't drink alcohol too often—neither did Cody—and both of us slurred our words. When I rose to visit the bathroom, I staggered and nearly fell. I stood before the toilet, swaying. Half my urine ended up on the floor. I didn't even bother flushing or zipping up, I just stumbled out of the bathroom with my cock hanging out of my boardshorts. Then I fell backward onto my bed.

Cody looked at me and rolled his eyes. "You're shitfaced, you know. You forgot to put your dick away."

The alcohol emboldened me, made me feel reckless. I looked down at my groin, then at Cody.

"Why don't *you* put it away for me?"

Cody made a face and snickered. "Are you making a pass at me?"

"Maybe," I said. "I'm so horny I could fuck a goat."

Cody made a bleating sound. "You sure know how to flatter a guy."

I jabbed at my mattress with a fingertip. "How about it?"

Cody drew a deep breath. He swung his feet to the carpet and placed his hands on his knees while my pulse pounded in my head. This was uncharted territory for me and Cody. We were best friends, sure. But what would he say?

Cody licked his lips. He looked at the door, then at me.

"Tell you what, Zach: I'll sleep in your bed and we can do whatever you'd like. Just don't tell anyone, okay?"

Holy crap . . .

My cock stiffened—it looked like a runaway banana—but I felt a tinge of guilt. Would I regret this once I sobered up? Was I taking advantage of Cody?

"Look," I said, "you don't have to do this."

Cody put his hands on his hips and a little smile played on his face.

"I *want* to, Zach. I really do."

Cody locked the deadbolt, engaged the door's security chain. He went to the bathroom and used the toilet. After flushing, he switched off the lights. Our drapes were thin. Glow from the motel's corridor lights entered the room, enough so I could see.

Cody stood beside my bed. Looking down at me, he loosened his shorts' drawstring and let them drop. I'd never seen Cody's cock before. It was long and pale, with a head shaped like a strawberry. His pubic bush was copper colored.

"Hey," Cody said.

I looked up into his face.

"How come I'm the only naked guy here?"

Chuckling, I shoved my boardshorts down my legs and kicked them away. Then I scooted over, making room for Cody. The bedsprings sighed when he lay beside me. His skin and hair smelled like pool chlorine. I lay on my back and Cody placed his cheek on my chest. He draped an arm across my waist, brought a knee to mine. His leg fuzz tickled my leg fuzz while he seized my erection in his fingers. He worked my foreskin back and forth. Then, shifting position, he took half my cock into his mouth and sucked it like a regular at Oleander Park.

I crinkled my forehead, thinking, *Huh?*

We were both drunk, of course. But something didn't feel quite right. I told myself, *This is far too easy.*

"Cody?"

He let my cock slip from his mouth. "What?"

"Have you done this before?"

He chuckled. "Lots of times."

"With who?" I said.

"You don't *want* to know."

"Of course I do."

"Are you sure?"

"Yeah, go ahead and tell me."

Cody let out his breath. "Zach, I was my brother's lover for the longest time."

Huh? Dean and Cody?

I felt like someone had punched me in the stomach. My vision blurred and a flash went off inside my head. My cock went limp as a dishrag. I pushed Cody away, sat up straight and flicked on the nightstand lamp. Cody's lips shone with spit. Both of us squinted in the brightness while our chests heaved.

"I don't believe this," I said. "How come you never told me?"

He raised a shoulder. "How come *you* never told me about Oleander Park?"

I fell onto my back and studied the popcorn ceiling, while questions flooded my brain. How long had Cody's affair with Dean lasted? What kind of sex acts had they performed and how often? Was Cody gay like me? Had he enjoyed lovemaking with his brother? Or had he simply submitted to Dean's will? Dean had dated girls in high school, real beauties. Had it all been a cover?

I didn't ask Cody about these things; they could wait. I had something more important on my mind.

"As long as we're getting secrets out of the way . . . ."

"What?"

"Tell me why you tried killing yourself? I want the truth this time."

Cody lowered his gaze and nodded.

"Turn off the light," he said. "Then I'll tell you."

Details of Cody relationship with his brother weren't all that complicated. When Cody had been fourteen, and Dean a year older, they experimented sexually while the Bartons vacationed in The Bahamas. The boys started with mutual masturbation, advanced to oral sex, and then anal.

"Dean was great in bed," Cody told me. "He'd done it with guys before."

Both brothers felt enthralled by their intimacies. They made a pact before returning to Florida: they'd become lovers, but no one, *nobody,* must know.

"Dean said if anyone found out, he'd have disaster on his hands. His reputation at school was important, he said. He had definite plans for his future: college, law school, and politics."

I lay there in darkness with Cody's head resting on my sternum. I didn't say a word.

"It was crazy," Cody said. "I'd pass Dean in the school hallway and he'd be talking with some girl he dated. He'd give me a wink and then I'd ask myself, 'What would the girl say if she knew?' Or I'd overhear Dean talking on the phone with his swim team buddies. He'd mention fucking this girl or that one, and then I'd recall him fucking *me* the night before."

I rubbed the tip of my nose. "Did you love Dean?"

"Of course I did. When he left for college, I thought I'd lose my mind. I kept calling him during fall semester—to see if I could come up to Gainesville for a visit—but he always said no 'cause he had no privacy there.

"Dean told me, 'Wait for Thanksgiving, little brother. I'll come home and we'll be together.'"

I twirled a lock of Cody's hair around my finger.

"Of course," Cody said, "Dean never made it home. When he died in that car trunk, I grew so depressed *I* wanted to die. Why go on living if I didn't have Dean in my life? I bought a length of rope, learned how to tie a noose from the Internet. It took me many months to work up the courage, but I finally did it. I figured death would bring me peace."

I shuddered, thinking of Cody hanging in his garage. "My mom told me there was an argument at your house, just before—"

"We had a blowup all right, on Christmas

Day, at the dinner table. My mom said it wasn't the same without Dean during the holidays, how we'd never understand the loss she 'felt in her heart.'

"It made me want to puke. I thought of the last time I'd made love with Dean, the night before he left for Gainesville. I told my mom, 'You didn't even *know* Dean. I was closer to him than you or Dad or anyone else. I'm the one who's suffering here.'

"My mom said something like, 'If you loved Dean you wouldn't have disappointed him so often. You never lettered in a sport; you never dated girls, were never popular like Dean. He felt embarrassed by you and your slouchy friends.'"

"When she said that, I . . . *exploded.* I stood up and threw a gravy boat across the room; it hit the wall and shattered. I said, 'Dean wasn't just my brother, Mom; he was my boyfriend. Do you hear me? He was my *lover.*'"

"Holy shit, Cody."

He chuckled deep in his throat. "Yeah: holy shit. At that point, the toothpaste was out of the tube. I'd disappointed my parents before, of course. But now they knew about me and Dean. They'd hate me forever, I knew, 'cause I'd destroyed their vision of who Dean was."

Cody rearranged his limbs and cleared his throat.

"I had no one left to love me, Zach. It was

time to die."

We lay there in silence for a bit, just breathing and thinking. I tried to imagine how lonely Cody must've felt Christmas Day and how badly he must've missed his brother.

Cody turned his head and looked at me.

"Any more questions?"

I shook my head.

* * * *

Cody and I didn't have sex at the beach motel. His revelation about his brother had shocked me so badly I couldn't *think* of touching Cody. I kept seeing visions of Cody and Dean in my head, the two of them surreptitiously making love while the rest of us remained clueless. I felt foolish, like the last guy in the room who's let in on the joke.

I imagined how Cody's parents must've felt when Cody thrust reality into their faces.

No wonder Cody couldn't return home.

During the remainder of our motel stay, Cody and I busied ourselves with walks on the beach, dining at fast food joints, and sunning ourselves by the pool. We bought a bottle of Canadian whiskey, courtesy of the UF boys, and our last two nights we drank the stuff mixed with ginger ale until we both passed out. We didn't discuss Dean or sex or anything remotely personal again.

I wasn't ready to.

* * * *

Spring break ended. We returned to school and our empty social life. Cody slept in his cot, I in my bed. We'd both been accepted to University of Central Florida, but attending there wasn't an option for Cody. At the dinner table one night, he said his parents had refused to pay for his education.

"I'm on my own after high school," he told me and my folks. "I'll find a job, attend community college part-time. It'll be okay."

My mom looked like she would cry. She told Cody, "You'll always have a home with us."

My dad nodded in agreement.

I signed up for fall semester at UCF. My folks sent them a deposit check. Then, during the last week of May, Cody and I walked across school's auditorium stage, looking ridiculous in our disposable caps and gowns. We both shook hands with the principal while my folks smiled and applauded. My dad took photos with his digital camera.

Cody's parents did not attend.

* * * *

In mid-August, Cody's mom died

unexpectedly, from an "aortic aneurysm." A blood vessel near her heart burst. In the space of ten minutes, she bled to death at the Bartons' country club, after collapsing on the putting green. Her obituary described her as a "loving wife and mother."

When Cody saw it in the newspaper, he shook his head.

"Bullshit," was all he had to say.

I went to the funeral only because I felt I should be there for Cody. We both wore starched shirts, neckties and khaki pants. The day was overcast, with a smell of rain in the air. At the Bartons' family plot, a breeze ruffled Cody's hair while they lowered his mom's casket into the ground. Cody, I noticed, wasn't observing the goings-on. Instead, he kept his gaze on Dean's headstone.

That night, lightning flashed outside my bedroom window. Thunder rumbled so hard the house shook. Cody's cot frame creaked.

"Zach, are you still awake?"

"Yeah, this storm's keeping me up."

"Me too; I can't sleep."

We decided to play cards. I flicked on my nightstand lamp and Cody joined me on my bed. We sat facing each other, legs crossed at our shins, both wearing boxer shorts. I shuffled the deck and dealt. Then we played gin rummy, arranging our tricks on the blanket, and saying little.

All summer long, Cody and I had power-raked people's Bahia lawns for cash. It was hard, sweaty work but paid well. In ten weeks we'd earned more than we could have bagging groceries an entire year. We were both tanned and fit, but skinny as ever. The muscles in my back and arms ached from the day's labors and I shifted my weight on the mattress, trying to get comfortable.

In a week, we'd return the power rake to the rental place. Then my dad would drive me to Orlando with my belongings and my college days would commence.

"Promise you won't pledge a fraternity," my mom had begged me.

I promised. What fraternity would pledge a guy with toothpick limbs and hair past his shoulders?

Now, in my room, Cody drew from the deck. "I'll miss you when you go," he said.

I nodded. How would it feel, not waking next to Cody each morning?

I told him, "At least you won't have to sleep on the cot. You'll like this bed."

After discarding, Cody looked up. "Will you do something for me, before you leave?"

I asked what.

He placed a hand on my knee and squeezed.

My eyebrows gathered. I looked at Cody's hand, then his face.

"Just once," he said. "It's been a rough day and I don't want to sleep alone."

I didn't know what to do. I thought of Dean's perfection. He'd been *way* out of my league; there was no way I could measure up to him and what he'd meant to Cody.

Say something.

"I'm not your brother," I told Cody. "I'm just a skater with zits."

Cody reached for my cheek and stroked it with his thumb. "It doesn't matter, Zach. You're my best friend; my *only* friend."

I hadn't touched a man sexually since my arrest. Already my cock was stiff and my pulse quickened.

Do it, stupid; do it for Cody.

Do it for you, too.

* * * *

We lay naked on my bed sheets, Cody and I, each guy gripping the other's erection. Our lips smacked and our tongues rubbed. My heart thumped while my belly did flip-flops. I kept running my fingers through Cody's hair, marveling at its thickness and texture. I kissed his eyelids, his forehead and the tip of his freckled nose. When he took my cock in his mouth and sucked the *glans*, I groaned so loud I'm surprised my parents didn't hear me.

Actually, I think they did.

Cody worked my cock with his tongue and lips. It felt heavenly. His mouth was warm and wet, so sensual. I shifted position so I could return the favor. Then we both slurped away. I loved the scent of Cody's crotch. How *different* this was from sex in Oleander Park. I was making love with my best friend, the guy who'd stood by me when no one else would.

What a fool I'd been, turning down Cody at the beach motel. Sure, I'd been angry because he'd hidden his sex life from me all those years, but hadn't *I* done the same to Cody? Now that he was in my bed, I couldn't get enough of him. I wrapped my arms around his waist and squeezed as hard as I could. I found Cody's lanky frame sexy; I liked touching him intimately.

Okay, I wasn't Dean Barton—I didn't have his looks or his athleticism—but at least I was there for Cody. Maybe I could offer him a small measure of what he needed. Not just tonight, but in the future, if he'd let me.

UCF's only a ninety-minute drive from

Clearwater. Maybe--

"Zach?"

"Yeah?"

"Will you fuck me?"

I greased my cock with lube from the nightstand drawer. Then I greased Cody's. He straddled me and sat on my erection. It was like nothing I'd ever experienced. I felt the clench of his pucker, the warmth of his gut when I entered him. Moonlight let me see the expressions on Cody's face while I thrust inside his body and he stroked himself. He looked drugged, as though he were far removed from reality.

A shiver ran through me when I came. My lungs pumped and my body jerked each time I shot. I closed my eyes while fireworks exploded in my head. Moments later, Cody cried out my name when he blew his load. His semen sprayed my chest and collarbone; it felt warm and viscous, teeming with his life force.

My cock still inside him, Cody bent at the waist and kissed my eyebrows. "That was wonderful, Zach. Is it okay if I tell you I love you?"Tears leaked from the corners of my eyes. Snot crowded my nose and my lips quivered. I felt completely overwhelmed.

This is all you've ever needed: Cody's love. Screw Oleander Park and screw the kids who bullied us at school. Screw Cody's parents, too. They never deserved him, but I do.

I've earned Cody's love by being his friend.

My mother called to me from beyond the bedroom door.

"Zach, are you and Cody okay?"

I wiped my eyes and sniffled. Then I cleared my throat.

"Yeah, Mom," I said.

"We're both fine."

Me and Shea

When I met Shea, I'd given up on love, but he changed that. Here's how it happened:

I had worked a long day, installing roof sheathing with a nail gun. In August it's hot in central Florida, especially when you're working outdoors, perched on trusses under a broiling sun. I pulled into my driveway with a twelve-pack of beer resting on the seat of my pickup, my skin sweaty and caked with sawdust.

I lived in a duplex: a building with two apartments sharing a common wall. The unit adjoining mine had been vacant for a few months, but now the "For Rent" sign was gone from the front yard. Next door, a Volkswagen van with a peace-sign sticker on its rear window sat on the driveway. The carport was full of cardboard boxes, most of them empty and scattered about. A fiberglass surfboard leaned against a wall.

I went over and knocked. This guy, nineteen or twenty, slender and a bit shorter than me, answered the door. His brown hair was arranged in Rasta braids; they grew to his shoulders. He wore nothing but boardshorts, A leather bracelet circled his ankle and his skin was deeply tanned.

"Moving in?"

He nodded, green eyes staring into mine. Stubble dusted his chin and jaw.

I jerked a thumb. "I'm Alex; I live next door."

He told me his name was Shea and we shook hands. His voice had a teenager's rasp.

I hoisted the twelve-pack. "Care for one?"

"Thanks, but I don't drink alcohol."

I squinted. *A surfer who doesn't like beer?*

He must have noticed my expression. "If I want to get high, I smoke weed. Hangovers hurt my performance."

"Huh?"

He pointed to his board. "On the waves."

I glanced at his upper body. His chest was defined, his shoulder muscles bulged and his belly was flat—a competition surfer's physique. *Of course,* I thought. When a Florida kid decides he'll make a living shredding waves, he comes to Brevard County to train at its many breaks: The Pier, Sebastian Inlet, Jetty Park, RCs and Second Light.

When I asked if he were in school, he nodded. "I start community college next week."

Hours later, when I watched TV, Shea knocked on my door. He clutched a manual can opener like my grandma owned when I was little. He asked, "Do you know how to operate this?"

I stifled a grin and followed him to his apartment. A can of ravioli, another of green peas, sat upon his kitchen counter. I demonstrated with the former, showing Shane how to position the opener's cutting blade on the lip of the can, how to squeeze the two handles and twist the knob. The device was ornery, so it took me a while to do the job.

While Shea struggled with the peas, I looked around. His place was just like mine: terrazzo floor, block walls, maple kitchen cabinets and Formica counter tops. In the living area were a bean bag chair, a portable TV atop a crate, and shelving constructed from plywood and concrete blocks. No drapes or blinds, nothing hung on the walls. A laptop computer, a drinking glass, and a stack of surfing magazines rested upon a card table, one with two folding chairs facing it.

Shea grimaced while he battled the can of peas. "You live alone?"

I nodded. "My wife and I split a few years ago."

He wrenched his lips. "That happens a lot, doesn't it?"

"What's that?"

"Divorce. Love doesn't last between people."

I didn't respond.

After succeeding with the opener, Shea dumped the peas into one saucepan, the ravioli into another. He placed both on stove burners, then set the temperature dials on "high". Leaning against his refrigerator, he crossed his arms and looked at me.

"You ever surf?"

"In high school, but not since. I work six-day weeks. By Sunday I'm too tired for paddling."

Shea asked about my job.

"I do carpentry—framing mostly. A little trim work as well."

"How old are you?"

I told him I was twenty-four.

His gaze slid over me like a clothes iron pressing a shirt. "You've got a nice build—strong shoulders. I'll bet you'd do fine on the water."

His remark embarrassed me and I looked at my feet.

"How come you're blushing?" Shea said.

I glanced up. "I'm not used to getting compliments."

He shrugged and didn't say anything.

A hissing sound came from the stove. The odor of singed pasta scented the kitchen. Burners beneath Shea's saucepans glowed bright orange and his peas were boiling over. He lurched across the room, grabbing the pans by their handles, only to drop them with a clatter and a curse. He flapped his hands, wincing, while I used a dishtowel as a hot pad, transporting his food to coils not in use.

After lowering his temperature dials to from "high" to "simmer", I asked Shea if he'd hurt himself.

He glanced into his palms. "A little, yeah."

I kept an aloe plant in my kitchen. I went next door and broke off a leaf, brought it to Shea. While he squeezed juice onto his fingers, I told him, "Invest in a potholder. And don't heat food on 'high'; you'll only scorch it."

He nodded, giving me a shy smile. "It's my first time keeping house."

"Your mom didn't teach you how to cook?"

He scowled and shook his head. "She left when I was seven."

"I'm sorry, I . . . ."

He said it was okay. Then he lowered his gaze and rubbed his belly. I sensed he felt ashamed by his mother's absence from his life.

"Look," I said, "I'm no whiz in the kitchen but I know a few things. If you have questions—about cooking or anything else—just ask."

He looked at me and smiled. Light from the ceiling fixture reflected in his teeth
.

"Thanks, Alex. I'll do that."

* * * *

I drove home from work, shortly after Shea moved in, and I spied a dinette—a wooden table and four matching chairs—sitting by a condominium's trash bin. Thinking of Shea and his lack of furniture, I stopped and placed the items in the bed of my truck.

At home, Shea's van rested on his driveway. When I knocked on his door he hollered, "Come in." Inside, I found him seated on a yoga mat in the lotus position, hands resting upon his knees. He was naked and I couldn't resist glancing at his groin. His cock was uncut, his ball sac shaved, and he'd trimmed his pubic hair to a patch no larger than two postage stamps.

Tearing my eyes from his genitals, I explained about the dinette, producing a hundred-watt smile on Shea's face.

"Alex, thanks so much. Let me get dressed and I'll unload the stuff."

His buttocks were round like melons; they jiggled as he walked to his bedroom. The flesh between his hips and knees, normally covered by his surf trunks, was hairless and white as cream. My cock stirred in my undershorts and my mouth felt like it was full of sawdust.

I should explain: During my junior year of high school a boy named Griffin, a classmate, became my lover. It began on a camping trip and lasted nearly six months, intensifying as it progressed. The sex was so good it almost hurt. Lying together in bed one afternoon, we declared our love for each other, promising we'd never separate. We even exchanged jewelry items. I gave Griffin a signet ring with my initials on it, and he gave me a gold chain I wore about my neck. We made plans to attend the university together, to share a dorm room. All of this occurred in secret. Nobody knew but us.

Toward the school year's end, Griffin's father was transferred by his employer to Seattle, some three thousand miles from Florida. When Griffin's family moved, our affair ended and I felt like somebody had cut out my heart and fed it to a dog. My school grades plunged along with my appetite. I lost weight and developed a rash on my face. When I wasn't at school, I stayed in my bedroom with the door closed, weeping at times, pining for Griffin till my stomach hurt.

I became so depressed I sliced my wrists with a box cutter; I nearly bled to death in our garage, earning myself a two-week stay in a psychiatric facility. My parents and a therapist tried to determine the source of my sorrow; they asked endless questions, but I wouldn't tell them about Griffin and me. After a while, they quit probing and left me alone.

While in the hospital, I promised myself I'd never love another guy; my loss of Griffin had been too painful. Thereafter, I dated girls off and on, playing the part of a straight man. I even married, as I'd told Shea, but it didn't last long. After the divorce, I admitted to myself I could not love a woman, not romantically, and at age twenty-one I swore an oath of abstinence. I would live a solitary existence.

Now, as Shea emerged from his bedroom, wearing only boardshorts, I glanced at the dark line of hair descending from his navel and into his waistband. I tried to memorize the way he'd looked moments before -- the bulge of his genitals and the curve of his ass. He entered the living room, brushing Rasta braids from his face with his fingers, and I smelled his body odor, something like a blend of shoe polish and cocoa butter.

I told myself, *Don't look at him, Alex. Don't.*

But I looked anyway.

* * * *

On a Saturday afternoon in early September, my air conditioner quit. When I called the landlady she said her repair guy didn't work weekends; I'd have to wait till Monday. The temperature was ninety at least, the humidity equally as high, and dampness gathered in my armpits. It would be a miserable evening.

I walked out my front door, just as Shea pulled into his driveway, surfboard attached to a rack on the roof of his van. He wore a black rash guard and boardshorts. Drops of seawater glistened in his braids.

"Have a good session?" I asked.

He nodded and grinned, loosening the straps securing his board. "Chest-high swells at Jetty Park. I was out there five hours, my arms are like noodles."

I spoke of my air conditioning problem.

"Hang out at my place," Shea said. "My unit works and I don't have plans for tonight."

I fixed dinner for us at Shea's: spaghetti and salad with Italian dressing. I drank Chianti, Shea iced tea. We sat at his dinette, listening to a local reggae station, while Shea spoke of his home life, up in New Smyrna Beach.

"There's my dad—he manages a hardware store—and my brother, who's fourteen and a computer geek. My grandma lives with us also."

Shea was shirtless. I asked about a tattoo on his shoulder, one the size of a stick of gum, the word "Sarah" appeared there in Gothic script.

When I asked about the tattoo, Shea said, "It's my mom's name."

"Where is she now?"

Shea looked into his plate and his voice cracked when he answered.

"We don't even know."

Shit.

I said, "My mom passed away five years ago—cancer. Then my dad remarried. He lives in Sarasota with his new wife and she doesn't care for my company. I see them at Christmas, that's about it."

"Brothers or sisters?"

I shook my head.

After dinner, I washed dishes while Shea dried and put them up We stood at the kitchen sink, side-by-side, our elbows and hips touching as we worked.

Shane spoke of his classes at school, his love for surfing, and how he admired his dad for raising Shea and his brother, all on his own. The subject of girls never arose.

"My dad's a devout Christian," Shea said; "a loving man."

"And you?"

He scratched his chest. "I try to follow Christ's teachings—do unto others and so forth—but I'm no angel."

We watched a movie on television. When it ended, I rose and stretched.

"Guess I'll call it a night," I said.

Shea looked up from his bean bag chair.

"Your place'll be an oven. Why not stay here?"

"Where would I sleep?"

Shea rose and turned off the TV. He pointed to the hallway. "My bed's a double; there's room for two."

My belly fluttered at the thought of sleeping next to him. I said, "You're sure you don't mind?"

"Heck, no. Come on."

He switched off lights. Then we took turns using the toilet.

In Shea's bedroom, a mattress lay upon the terrazzo floor, equipped with a sheet, two pillows and a thin blanket. A chest of drawers hugged one wall. Several clothing items hung in a closet with bi-fold doors. Shea extinguished the ceiling fixture, but moonlight entered through a window. After my eyes adjusted I saw things quite clearly.

He pointed to the bed. "I'll take the side by the window."

I nodded, keeping still, unsure what I should do.

Shea untied the drawstrings of his boardshorts. Dropping them to his ankles, he kicked them aside. After scratching his nuts, he sank to the mattress. He lay upon his back with his fingers laced behind his head, his elbows jutting. He shot me a quizzical look.

"Are you waiting for an invitation?"

I smiled and shook my head. *What did he mean by that remark?*

Ditching my t-shirt and jeans, I kept my boxer shorts on. I reclined beside Shea, my head resting on a pillow. The blanket lay bunched at our feet. Our hips and shoulders nearly touched. Again, I smelled

Shea's hair and skin. I glanced down at his cock, it lay draped across one thigh, the foreskin crinkly and dark.

Shea shifted his weight and his knee met mine.

"You can touch me if you'd like, Alex; it's okay."

His remark, so direct and clear, took me by surprise. I lay motionless, chest rising and falling, gaze fixed upon the ceiling. *He wants you, stupid. Go ahead* . . .

Shea placed a hand on my shoulder. "What is it?"

I said, "I don't know if I can do this." I explained about Griffin, describing my suicide attempt and all. It took ten minutes, and Shea remained silent the entire time. I told him, "I might seem like a tough guy, but I'm easily hurt."

Shea drew closer; he draped an arm across my chest and pressed his temple to my shoulder. His braids tumbled here and there while his breath swept my skin. He said, "You're all alone in this world, aren't you?"

I nodded.

"I won't hurt you, Alex. I promise."

My heart hammered. I felt overwhelmed by the situation, afraid it might lead to trouble. Shea was five years younger than me, a college kid; we had little in common. And what was it he'd said? *Love doesn't last between people.* If we became boyfriends it would end badly, as with Griffin, and I wouldn't be able to stand it; I'd go crazy again.

I pulled away from Shea. Sitting up, I turned my back to him and reached for my shorts.

"What are you doing?" he said.

"Going home."

"Alex, don't. Stay here with me."

I slipped into my shorts, then I rose and scooped up my shirt. When I glanced down at Shea, his forehead was furrowed and his eyes looked sad.

I told him, "You don't understand; I can't get involved, not with you or anybody else."

I left, then, making my way through the dark apartment, telling myself, *What a fool you are; what a chickenshit. You passed up sex and maybe something more. Other people recover from heartbreak. Why can't you?*

I emerged from Shea's place and the muggy outdoor air hit my face like a wet sponge. Crickets chirped while air conditioners whirred at nearby homes. A car passed on the street, its muffler growling. I sat in a lawn chair on my little front porch, sweating and craving a cigarette, even though I hadn't smoked in several years.

What was wrong with me? Griffin had left Florida seven years before. Why couldn't I overcome my grief?

I slept fitfully, partly because of the humidity, but mostly because of Shea. I kept picturing him naked in the moonlight, his knee touching mine. He was sexy and intelligent and sensitive—everything I could want in a boyfriend. He had reached out to me. Then, like an idiot, I had rejected him. And for what reason? A fear I might someday lose him?

When I woke the next morning, Shea's van was not in his driveway. I assumed he'd gone surfing, but by dinnertime he still had not returned and I began to worry. I kept walking to my front window, looking out, wondering where he might be. It wasn't till nine or so that I heard the mutter of his engine.

I waited ten minutes, running through my mind what I planned to say. Then I walked next door. He answered wearing a Hawaiian shirt and cargo shorts. I trembled when I looked at him, my voice cracked when I told him hi.

He didn't reply; he only looked at me.

"Where were you all day?"

He glanced over my shoulder. "In New Smyrna; I went to see my family."

I nodded and studied my feet. "Look, I'm sorry about last night; I shouldn't have—"

"Alex, you're not the only person who's been hurt by a loved one. My *mother* left me, for Christ's sake, but that won't stop me from loving another person. Sometimes you've got to take a chance."

I looked at Shea and nearly cried because he was so beautiful. My voice quivered when I spoke. "Promise me you're serious, that it's not only for sex."

His hands went to his hips. He snorted and shook his head. "I've wanted you since the day we met, when you showed me how to use a can opener. Remember?"

I nodded, fists clenched at my hips.

"I tossed you hints, gave you opportunities, but you missed every one."

I thought of his compliment in the kitchen, of the day he'd let me view him naked. I recalled our touching while we'd done dishes the night before. What an idiot I was.

When I asked if I could come in, Shea nodded.

He said, "Sure, of course," and then the tension drained from my body.

Once inside I did not hesitate: I wrapped my arms about Shea's neck and pulled him to me, inhaling his scent. He rested his chin on my shoulder; his braids pressed against my cheek and his arms encircled my waist.

"Want to try again?" he whispered.

I nodded.

In his bedroom, we undressed in moonlight, saying nothing, just looking at each other. Our cocks were stiff; they bobbed before us. I went to Shea and crooked an arm about his neck. I pulled him to me, feeling his boner press against mine. He kissed my cheek, took my ear lobe between his front teeth and nibbled. I turned my head and our mouths joined. Shea's tongue pried my lips apart, seeking my tongue. His stubble scraped my chin while his breath steamed against my upper lip.

After sinking to the mattress, we kissed like a pair of love-starved kids. I toyed with Shea's braids; they were thick like his cock. Placing a hand on his pectoral, I pinched his nipple and made him groan. His skin felt warm and inviting, smooth to the touch. My hand traveled south, over his rippled belly, through his little patch of pubic hair, to his swollen cock. I took it in my hand and peeled back the foreskin. I teased the head with my thumbnail, drawing fresh moans from Shea.

Simultaneous cock-sucking had always been my favorite sex act with Griffin. When I requested this from Shea, he responded eagerly. Shifting his position on the mattress, he took my cock into his mouth, forming a seal with his lips. He polished the underside of my cock with his tongue while his head bobbed. It felt heavenly and I groaned. I ran my hands through his braids, massaging his scalp and thrusting my hips.

Shea had not showered since morning and his genitals smelled gamey, an arousing scent. His ball sac tasted salty when I licked it. I nibbled his foreskin with my teeth, tugging at it here and there before slipping his cock into my mouth.

How I've missed this feeling, this intimacy.

Shea's erect cock was a whopper. I gagged at first, trying to get it all down my throat. But as soon I relaxed, I found a rhythm. I slurped away like a child with a snow cone. We went at it like this for a good fifteen minutes, giving each other pleasure until Shea lifted his face from my groin.

"Alex, will you fuck me?"

He furnished a condom and I took him on his back with his legs hiked, his knees touching his shoulders.

"Go easy," he told me. "It's been a while."

His hole was tight; it went into spasms when I entered him. Twice, I had to pull out before he was able to relax and handle my penetration. I'd forgotten how delicious anal sex was: the thrusting, the strength and tension a man's body offered. We both sweated and our skins smacked as we rocked on the mattress. Shea's hand pumped his cock while he gazed at the ceiling, his lips parted, moonlight reflecting off his teeth. His breath huffed, as did mine.

My cock throbbed inside him, and then I flooded the condom with my seed. At the same time, Shea's cock shot jizz onto his chest and belly, a series of spurts making his body jerk. He cried out my name and Jesus' too.

I couldn't help myself; I wept.

I remained inside Shea, holding him while my tears fell upon his neck. Life had been so lonely since Griffin's departure, but now I sensed my sadness would lessen. I felt as if I'd taken a long and solitary journey, but now I'd returned home, to find Shea and all that he offered.

I held him tightly, kissing his cheek while our whiskers rubbed.

I whispered, "thank you," over and over again like a mantra. Not just to the boy in my arms, but to God as well, for giving me a second chance.

I thanked Him for giving me Shea.

About the Author:

Martin Delacroix's stories have appeared in over two dozen anthologies. He has published several novels and four, single-author anthologies. Read about these, and other Martin Delacroix publications, at www.martindelacroix.com.

Martin lives on a barrier island on Florida's Gulf Coast.

www.ingramcontent.com/pod-product-compliance
Lightning Source LLC
Chambersburg PA
CBHW062114040426
42337CB00042B/2285